ACTING LIKE A GIRL

By the same author:

Projected on the Wall (2016)
Who Sleeps at Night (2017)
The Orlando Files (2018)

ACTING LIKE A GIRL

SANDRA RENEW

RECENT
WORK
PRESS

Acting like a girl
Recent Work Press
Canberra, Australia

Copyright © Sandra Renew, 2019

ISBN: 9780648404224 (paperback)

 A catalogue record for this book is available from the National Library of Australia

All rights reserved. This book is copyright. Except for private study, research, criticism or reviews as permitted under the Copyright Act, no part of this book may be reproduced, stored in a retrieval system, or transmitted in any form by any means without prior written permission. Enquiries should be addressed to the publisher.

Cover photograph: Copyright © Tikka Wilson, 2018
Cover design: Recent Work Press
Set by Recent Work Press

recentworkpress.com

for Tikka (and Hue).
You know who you are.
You know what you do.

Contents

Her own personal catastrophe	1
Paying attention	2
summer queer	3
her beauty in androgyny …	5
girls who are taken by flannies	6
She knows a boy	7
Not very quiet	8
it's all in the walk (1960s)	9
Transformer	10
Keeping order in the social order	11
… as many as it takes	12
Sometimes still …	13
Robbie Burns may not have been completely right …	14
How do we imagine what we can't imagine?	15
postal survey—not binding, not compulsory	16
From the point of view of the sea	17
Set in concrete	18
Gecko	19
Sea Horse Ball	20
Dog	21
High point of the season	22
Toad Princes	24
to lesbian (i)	25
Situation	26
there's a small farm	27
Edit	28
She can only be this woman because she's not this woman	29
Whatever she is, she wants to be Wesley Hall	30
Harley	31
Homing	32
He went to the beach at Brighton and shot himself	33
Kings Cross at home	34
Here it's difficult to tell the difference	35
St Kilda 1972	36
peripatetic affair	37

glass-bottomed boat	38
Gay	39
CAMP	40
Measuring Denier	41
Scorpio to Venus: Love song 1977	42
Plot	44
Use a very sharp knife	45
Getting through Sunday	46
from the get-go	47
Nancy revisited	48
Afterword	51

Her own personal catastrophe

Trust what I tell you.
I am here to describe
one of the greatest discoveries
that has ever been made.
She urges her horse, with one leap,
into the burning pile of logs.
The rope dancer dances upon a rope,
holds in his upraised hand the Great Bear and the Pole Star.
The fire sparks fountains to the sky.
The world turns and turns.

Paying attention

She's paying attention
like the fox
trembling at the burrow mouth
one paw raised
before the early sun.

She's paying attention
like the magpie
poised on the high branch
on duty,
spring nest protection.

She's paying attention
like a girl
in uniform trousers
barbered hair
new military   new gender

summer queer

the holidays are locked and loaded
Best Book lists are piled high on bedside tables
cricket will be over when it's over,
tennis balls *klock, klock, klock*
on grass and clay and rough dirt courts wherever ...

girls from the women's-land collectives *(what are ya?)*
in town all winter with their off-season girlfriends
drove north for the summer weeks ago
... hat and sarong, and serious land cultivation tools
wrapped in clear plastic,
thrown into a sweating sedan with dogs in the back

homeowners
drive to the beach,
ceding the field to Summer Nats' screaming *(fucking dyke)* thunder
    revs, wet T-shirt competitions (banned),
alcoholic fumes mixing with HK-8000 burn out fuel,
trespassing in bush gardens to chunder in dusty grass

two girls
with winter legs
try peroxide
to bleach the stubble
before they strip to sunbake

summer queer,
dazzled by sun on water,
glittering silica sand,
what game are we playing?

stripped down for volley ball, how fast is slow?
splashing, waist-deep, in waves barely surf, how light is the glimmer
of recognising?

It's no holy day, timing out the sojourner …

promenading
between seaweed clumps
and stranded jellyfish
she imagines her body
re-shaped in convex lenses

her beauty in androgyny, she is all desire, desires all, shares herself under the gaze with all genders, is all beauty

hands in pockets
she strides, but slowly …
tilts her hat—
on the bridge out of town
spits, thumb cocked for a lift

girls who are taken by flannies

when she thinks about it, bold checks fade and bleed at the edges
warm cotton softens   spineless collar points curl
small fraying starts where the cuffs roll back   to join the sleeves—

girls who are taken by flannies
learn to give as good as they are given   use the cold stare
fists ready the f word little finger curled making a point

giving out what they're not
freedom from the drag of frock   family manners
and demands to change for dinner

wrestling the spare from inside the ute tray
tire iron used more freely than a flat iron   dropping the jack down
   spinning her wheels in the gravel edge of the road metal

girls who are taken by flannies are wall flowers   around the edges
B&S balls leave them outside
in the cold   smoking   with a warm beer
waiting for the drive home

She knows a boy

She knows a boy
who sucked his sleeves, nibbled and mouthed with a nervous tic
swallowed the threads until the checks
were eaten to the elbow
and the collar exposed as fraud—
flannie eating is a boy thing

Not very quiet

In the time of Germaine Greer
I had a quiet New Year,
went to the neighbour's place.

She had a crate of champagne
and a jelly wrestling pool.

it's all in the walk (1960s)

she looks like a boy, it's hard to tell
she walks like a boy, throws like a boy when its cricket
on the school oval
her pin ups are the West Indies cricket team
(especially Wesley Hall)

she tackles and kicks like a boy, as if she's a boy,
in the Under 12's Saturday team, she's the one they want
on the wing, she barracks for Geelong in the League

when she's called on it, she fights like a boy, all fists and elbows,
when she's got a harasser down,
she sinks in the boot, kicks in the guts, to finish them off, like a boy

she swings an axe like a boy, sinks a star picket in four mallet strokes
in *Gone with the Wind* she wants to be Rhett,
for dress-ups with a girl-friend she chooses black,
in the op-shops she picks trousers and jackets, and combat boots

she walks like a boy, acting like a boy
at graduation she's in drag, heels, frock and handbag, (for her mother)
she meets a boy, acting like a girl, acting like a boy

he plays like a girl, acting like a girl
he dances like a girl, cocktail frock in sequins, bosoms,
over-lacquered hair, delicate footwork, tentative hands,
fingers saying *I'm fragile*

her suits, his frocks
using her body, like a girl, like a boy

Transformer

her family cannot pass on how she should be ... she's seven ...
her mother makes her a princess tutu she doesn't want,
kitchen table audience insisting on pirouettes she refuses to do,
she rides with her father on the tractor,
tutu bouffant over riding boots ...

she's fourteen ... her taffeta skirt is a good start
(twisted, woven fabric suitable for use in ball gowns, wedding dresses)
(and corsets and corsetry)—

fashion advice in the *Women's Weekly*, satins and shot silk, tulle and
netting suitable for tutus (here we go again) and bridal dress veils...

standing on a chair, her mother pursing her mouth around pins,
bodice darts, ruches
before she goes away to Teachers College there are sequins,
bridesmaids dress with v neck pleats
sexy A-line drawing the eye to the cleavage
(she doesn't make a big thing of her cleavage)

the change is startling, bouffant beehive teased to splitting point,
changing to layered, then razor cut, then number 4 clippers
(no ends in sight)
spiked with gel and hair putty

party dress transmogrifies into *Blundstones*, waistcoats, *Sobranie Russians*,
an unlikely transformation unless
you had thought she was going through a phase, a phrase,
unless you had been watching her, unless
unless you were her watching herself metamorphing
a phrase, shapeshifting

Keeping order in the social order

Virginia writes Vita as Orlando
love writing love, writing a love story
of Virginia and Vita
a story of women and three centuries of love
of Violet and Vita, in love with Orlando
how many lives does a girl have to live?

... as many as it takes

Monique Wittig
she re-reads the text of the world
as a lesbian text
through the eyes of heroes with unstable bodies
she glitters in the sun   read me as a lesbian

Luce Irigaray
writes woman as difference   the gap between the actors of the world
she writes woman outside the control of the world
first as nothing, then as everything
first as silence, then the subversion of silence

Julia Kristeva
Kristeva makes heroes of us all
she insists we contradict   resist
and as exile and dissident
use all spaces as lesbian
live as metaphor

Hélène Cixous
Cixous has written me a letter
she writes of Tancredi
to me as Tancredi
and speaking for myself
I am in love with Tancredi

Jacques Derrida
the dyke loves Derrida
he teaches me the fancy dancing
steps and choreography
multiplicity of dances
to dance myself—play myself, playing myself

Sometimes still ...

Sometimes she still finds herself
in company where she's a dyke in a tea-cup,
stirring salt into the brew of heterosexuality,
with nothing to offer for the offence
of her existence, the taste
of dyke in the tea-cup,
a sip of dissent.

Robbie Burns may not have been completely right ...

Oh wad some power the giftie gie us
To see oursels as others see us!
It wad frae mony a blunder free us,
And foolish notion.

Dear Robbie Burns,
As a lapsed Presbyterian, I think it is sometimes better not to know how we are seen by our friends and enemies.
Sometimes a too good, goody-two-shoes Presbyterian could do with entertaining
some foolish notions—
it is good to realise that most blunders, while posing a temporary hold-up
or trip up
do not signify the end of the world as we know it.
        Best regards
                Dyke (origin unknown)

How do we imagine what we can't imagine?

The sail-fish and the iguana give the lie to the science before Galapagos.
They are the best case.
They provide the proof that allows knowledge over belief and ignorance, imagination over law.

So, in the waters off Galapagos
the iguanas swim
and the fish fly.

postal survey—not binding, not compulsory

they worry and fret before they bang the short post into the soft soil
of the front garden bed, beside the waiting letter-box …
stand back, look at it together, wonder if the rainbow sign can be
seen clear enough for passers-by and slow suburban drivers—

in the days following, they double-lock doors and windows,
buy a chain for the garden gate,
listen in the evenings for the meaning of noise,
make convoluted arrangements to never leave
the dog home alone and vulnerable.

From the point of view of the sea

listen
in tropical water a manatee is breathing—

refugee from storm-fed ocean currents
manatee congregate in tribal mass
wherever shallow coastal warmth kisses and soothes

south of here an ice mountain is exploding
two hundred thousand tonnes of iceberg slips free,
floats north into shipping lanes

ice on metal ... listen ... nudges container ships carrying
fuel and food to the island
moves with the unpredictability
of flotsam, not yet described as worthless.

Set in concrete

In nineteen sixty
a bird steps in concrete ...
just before
or just after
Barry and Cheryl,
using a stick to write neatly
in capital letters,
cement their relationship ...

Gecko

inside the room she waits to die
the gecko watches, calls

outside, under the pergola
we argue about the church, a service religious or secular
her aversion to the influence of religion
the question of where to hold a wake—
my mother dies

I remember her voice, her poetry on the radio
neither are light—
like the songs she would have scoffed at
Won't you stay?

she knows that light is frivolous, dark is serious
words are both light and dark

it seems only the gecko speaks to her directly

Sea Horse Ball

We keep our breasts in a boudoir drawer—
high heels, embroidery, yellow satin,
a full skirt, décolletage, diamanté

we get glammed up ...
hats, boas, foundation garments,
scarves, lipsticks, silky fabrics

we see each other, breathe in our scents
perfumes of cross-dressed sisters
makeovers, takeovers, star crossed secrets

Dog

She rang me one night from a two-star motel on the main street of a small country town in far north Queensland—the dog, which had travelled with her so far, had run off, out into the rain.
Leaning in the doorway until the tropical storm had passed over the cane-fields, she could still hear the downpour when it reached the base of the mountain.

But there was no sign of the dog, and she wanted to move on—
Should she leave the dog out there? After all, it had gone of its own accord, she said.

I could hear the drag of her cigarette, the slap-slap as she flattened mosquitos, drain pipe dripping, and an echoing thud she said was a cane-toad as she kicked it away against the fibro wall.
Just wait for the dog. What else do you have to do?

High point of the season

We didn't do it for the politics or religion. We did it because we were mad with the heat and tension, and we just *went troppo*.

Every afternoon we waited as the monsoon built up, anticipation and tension, and then fizzled away leaving us with nothing ... not a cool breeze, a rain drop or even a degree or two drop in temperature.

The two of us, unemployed, itinerant, were living in a disintegrating wooden cottage on the banks of Ross Creek. Window panes held in place by thumb-tacks and balanced in rotting wood frames, stuck open to the wild life and weather.

Mould in our bike helmets. Bats in the mango tree. Mangoes rotting in the uncut grass. Cane-toads waiting for an open door. Our interest in living was reduced to subdued drinking sessions of Bundy, if we had found a few hours work, or warm tinnies of XXXX, otherwise.

We left the bikes covered in hope of the rains arriving in the night. Come morning, a heart-stopping tarantula, in the folds of the tarp, would leap awake, with all legs going, to fling itself at the arm connected to the dry-stiffened cloth.

Our front porch gave on to a view of the railway yards. Coal trains going through to the port, day and night, were lit by those blurred orange standing lights reflecting off clouds of jostling, frenzied insects.

There was a lay-by for the long-haul B-double trailers beside us on the cross street. Refrigeration running while drivers went into town for the pub made us angry and desperate. Often a three-trailer combo upped the ante in that particularly aggravating generator-whine sound-scale in our humidity-maddened brains.

In the deep, mango-scented shade, with the blue plastic basin and dipper between us, we started with the kitchen scissors, hacking and sawing until our heads felt bristled and uneven to the fingers. Careful, but unsteady with audacity, we lathered and shaved, using a whole packet of Bic disposable razors, the water suddenly cool on our bare skulls.

Toad Princes

we were out that night in the Holden ute
road through the cane-fields slippery as all get out
downpour roaring and closing down the viewing distance to a few feet
steam struggling to rise off the tarmac against the force of rain

the toad count rose, all those potential princes, under the wheels,
high beam picking them out, stunned but sanguine,
on both sides of the white line
while she gunned the engine, veered and swerved and yahoo-ed
every time we got one,

squashed flat, bloody for a moment but then guts
sluiced away as storm-water—
hanging out the windows to make the body count
sodden, dripping, high on adrenalin and the 'us' of it
empty half-bottle of Bundy flat on the floor in the footwell

to lesbian (i)

to lesbian ...
suicide bomber—experienced
closet evangelical
library open weekdays 10 am to 4 pm
alleges non-consensual, *teaching you to be a proper woman*, sexual assault

there's something about the contradictions
if true is a weapon used against her—

to lesbian (verb) (ii)

I write as a lesbian. Read me as a lesbian.

Dyke

An embankment for restraining the waters of the sea or a river
A ditch
A ridge or bank of earth as thrown up in excavating
A causeway
An obstacle, barrier
A tabular body of igneous rock which cuts across the structure of adjacent rocks or cuts massive rocks; formed by intrusion of magma
Colloq. A lavatory
To furnish or drain with a dyke
To enclose, restrain, or protect by a dyke: to dyke a tract of land
Colloq. a lesbian [origin unknown]

dyke is all these things, at least all these things.

Situation

Cixous has written me a letter.
She writes to me, and, as a lesbian reader, I answer.

When I write, it's because I have received a letter.
As reader, I author the writer.

The writer writes from possibilities,
a conscious writer, a visible writer, I make clear to the world
to whom you are writing, and as whom I respond.

Being out and visible, out and present and speaking for myself,
speaking up for myself, speaking from my body, from my lesbian body,
writing from the freedom of Tancredi and the multiple, plural possibilities.

Notwithstanding
we have a situation!
Does she cause it,
or fix it?
Or both?
We have a situation.
She brings all her issues
to bear.

She lights her pipe
sucking in the smoke
she holds the match again to her pipe.
She counts the dresses hanging
 in her cupboard ... none.

There is no keeping order in the social order
and, on the whole,
in those days,
dykes made disappointing daughters.

there's a small farm

there's a country road
you've just discovered lesbian
in a heavy Oxford dictionary, school chanting *lezzo lezzo lemon*
imagine you're a lesbian

imagine you are reading
some Great Poets' collected works of Poetry...
struggling through the poems, running thumbnail down the index
can you find a lesbian?

there's a road
a greyhound bus, a highway
a big city ... imagine you're a lesbian
can you see it as a lesbian, gay city, streets of queer?

tell me who you see
where she went, and why

there's a night club, Ruby Red's,
a closet burst wide open
a record, Dusty Springfield pop song
there is dancing and there's *dancing*

there's an attitude, an incident that follows,
a policeman, policy of government
there's a broken law, a court case,
headlines in the news, definitely a lesbian

Edit

It is night in the rotting mangoes and sticky tar of mid-summer, our energy so low and heat-sapped it is demanding proof of life. I again look for *defenestrated* in the tea-stained *Macquarie Dictionary New Budget Edition*. The word has lived since 1618 but it's not in there.

I have an undercurrent of irritation that he, the immediate subject of the action, more than likely deserves being *defenestrated*—providing a disincentive for his future assumptions.

A momentary sizzle as one of us drops a butt into a XXXX stubbie and the dying thread of used cigarette smoke teases between us. There are no possums in this neighbourhood but I've seen a rat before on the powerlines: balanced between the dead flying fox and old, equally dead underpants.

I stay beside the window, my arms, bare in a navy work singlet, absorbing neon. If I shut the window it is less likely to invite a defenestration but the possibilities for a slowly wrought castration remain high.

She can only be this woman because she's not this woman

She shimmers in a cocktail dress of stupendous blue
prefers stilettos to a pinet heel
undulates, pirouettes
flaunts her legs and public walks
like she was born to
her dress moulds her hips, nips in the waist
threads flow of warp and weft catching light

she's settling in to get her hair done
make-up, make-over
whatever she is, she's not this woman—
she can only be this woman

Whatever she is, she wants to be Wesley Hall

    She has a pin-up on her bedroom wall
    of Angela Davis
but she wants to be Wesley Hall
whatever she is, she wants to be him—
she's not black, she's not from Barbados, she's not tall,
she knows nothing about cricket.

    It's Angela they sing about, the Rolling Stones,
    Bob Dylan, John Lennon
    they sing her from Hoover's *10 most wanted*,
    from fugitive to solitary in the penitentiary—
    dangerous and intellectual, communist and activist
    her big, big hair says Reagan, and she's the owner of the gun

but she wants to be Wesley Hall
she wants his grace in the air,
as the ball leaves his hand
she wants to use her body like that, muscled-strong, heroic
his cricket whites casual, flamboyant,
whatever she is, she wants to be him

Harley

I don't remember how I was taught this—the antidote to the cold is work, put your back into it! Years at the wood heap, swinging an axe or splitter, building shoulders the envy of Navratilova or Stosur. Looking wrong in taffeta or chiffon, thighs and calves making dress-up shoes look like drag—callouses, bruises, scrapes and splinters, dirt ingrained, skin stained.

Rolling the *Drum fine cut* with one hand, an affectation, true, *Tally Ho* cigarette papers *licked by millions*. Drag and hold, smoking the durry down to the stained and soggy roach, pinched between yellowed thumb and forefinger, strands of loose tobacco stuck to my lip, and, depending on the depleted state of the kitty, pulling the last strands from the bitter end to roll again.

On the footpath café in weak winter sun, a woman being wooed, her face like a carved mask; dreadlocked youth being handcuffed; hippie in a long, faded tie-dyed skirt, earbuds appearing from beneath dyed split ends, saying *shit shit shit!* old man in grey suit pants, no jacket, eating two desserts.

> standing beside the Harley at the stop light
> earth trembles
> air moves like muscle

Homing

the love
                in your veins
        is otherwise

sweeping
            terror
                            for me

all tragic
      tangle
            the warm dark

pitiless
      we bless
            an army

pay back threefold

            I may die
homing

He went to the beach at Brighton and shot himself

lift me down
        your work cut out
                sullen, sluggish lamp

wreaths hard behind still
                crashed

powder singed young, reckless
                left alone

squandered wife long dead, woman grown and wed
share short span

smoking shadows
    pall   bed   grave
chance

Kings Cross at home

Spine text from a brass plaque set into footpath in Kings Cross Sydney

Gawd	whose ever god you are
Strike	it does not strike
Me	me
Dead	that you actively, specifically, want me dead—
Is	is it more than just a thought
That	that in our collective
Supposed	supposed sanctity
To	of life to
Be	be extinguished carelessly
A	on a whim, even godly, but definitely of phobic man's
Man	makes no sense although it's man
Or	against man or more
A	commonly at home against a woman
Woman?	who is struck — is she that woman?

Here it's difficult to tell the difference

If	if, as supposed, s/he is a woman bashed
It's	it's confusing for the men in blue attending, warning flashing
Too	too hard to see finally see through to two men, one too
Feminine	overstated feminine
To Be	immediately to be questioned
A	a question mark held over
Woman	exclaimed, claimed a woman
It's	it's too far to leap
Got	unless you got it early
To	twigged to the fishnets, slinky gown, sparkly make up
Be	a 'being Cleopatra'
A	a new wave Kylie
Bloke	a bloke by another name

St Kilda 1972

This Is The Show / Green Dragon Lounge

This body defeats her, even in the skirt and blouse
In afternoon haze, but still broad daylight
Taking stock of the bar, checking swilling customers
She's come up short, not only in the float

Generally speaking, she's not hailed as a looker, safely not a
Rozzer spying for police but often called a lezzo
Every man in the bar, every all day drinker,
Every after-work walk-in grey or brown suit
Notices the *real dog*, not pretty, obvious she's not a hooker

Darlin' same again but quicker
Razzing, not in a nice way, reflex reflux, sour taste
And the mob closes to the cut-off, six pm
Glasses high, *here girlie, same again but double*
One big round before the swill is closed
Not missing out because of you, ya wet-week slow

Look, I'll glass him for ya luv shoving to the front
One crack on wood the glass rim shatters
Ugly, sharp, instant weapon, eye gouger, face cut
No-one in the bar wants this, the mob parts around him
Girlie, they're blokes   they wanta see ya tits
Expectorates into the bucket, *doncha get it?*

peripatetic affair

a letter
                sent

unexpected   my vision gone

night everlasting, I am floating

all hurry
                faintly daunt
                              haunt

eager waste   season's fancy

eternal journal
                I doubt

glass-bottomed boat

trying to work out if this woman is The One
is like wanting to time-travel to be sure of it

like wanting a glass-bottomed boat
when all you have is a scratched and dented tinnie
and this time, now

in the tang of tidal mangroves looking for someone else's crab trap
hoping for an illicit catch of muddies

bare brown toes hooked over the gunwhale
lying back
in the still shade and drift

Gay

it was an idea and it came to her like galahs
bursting out of a mulga canopy
pink and grey, shrieking their tits off

she knew that with the stripes and flashes, colour clashes
her shorts were gay, and her favourite shirt
faded, labourers' grey, wrinkled deformed collar, never worked

the dress, in her size, smoky blue
shirtwaist nylon materialised one day
hanging on a wire hanger behind her bedroom door

it was more than a suggestion, a finger point—
the dress was a challenge, a dare
a deal breaker

the dress, it's just not me she said
it could be you her girl friend said
if you made an effort   if you cared

so when the idea crashed out of her reality
it was so beautiful and water-in-the-desert cool
that she gasped, and grasped and held it

the dress could stay   and she could go

CAMP
Campaign Against Moral Persecution Brisbane

It was the last twilight of summer but it did not appear to be the end of something. She dresses as a woman dressing as a dyke, coming out. One day she will grow up and, going out, she will dress as a woman being a woman going out.
For now, she's a boy/woman, interesting, ambiguous, definitely dyke.

ASIO agents are on hand, as usual, in the alley at the back entrance, photographing people as they enter the thin, steep stairway. The heavy wooden door on the main street, with the discreet brass plaque and street number, is locked, for security.

Trains can be heard from Roma Street station, the evening departure for Townsville and Cairns in the far north—*you can come with us, home to the country, every evening at this time*—goods vans shunting, doors crashing closed on all the travelling baggage and things you can't leave behind.

At the top of the stairs, a double knock, peephole slides back, dyke credentials open the door.

Tonight they're painting the backroom lesbian lavender, a little space with a sloped ceiling, bloke free, no queens, pretty boys stay out. Here is theirs, their centre, their own moving from the edges.

Who has an ASIO file with photographs? Who is spotted in spray can paint? Who will go to work tomorrow dressed as a woman going to work? Who will get fired? Who has the 1970s bruises and tattoos? Who thinks she is making the whole fucking place better?

Somewhere between Joh Bjelke Petersen's Queensland and Ellen DeGeneres' *Ellen* we talked our way in from the borders and onto the streets, found our self-respect and fought back.

Measuring Denier

At the second typing and shorthand session at the *June Dally Watkins School of Deportment and Grooming*, she was told the dress code was indeed a dress: a modest secretarial dress, and stockings—with the suitable denier for an office environment.

Low denier could be sheer but was delicate and easier to run. If you wore sheer hosiery to work, it was safer wearing 15 to 20 deniers. Under 10 deniers was ultra-sheer and not for those who bought their own hosiery. A boss, a bloke, may buy you stockings if you excelled at accurate shorthand, speed-of-light typing, and legs-together deportment, although *that* relationship was never made clear.

So, she wrestled the heavy Suzuki GT550, over the Milton hill and down into Auchenflower in the heavy tropical downpour that occured most evenings at the tail end of rush hour. The monsoon was chucking it down, the bike skating on water running between her tires and the tar, dribbles leaking down inside her jacket, her visor fogging up.

At the take-away, she backed the bike into the kerb, kicked it onto the lean-in stand and took off her helmet.

As she waited at the counter for her Chiko roll in the designer paper bag that went transparent as the grease soaked in (one of 40 million to be sold in the seventies), and a tub of Neapolitan ice-cream (mulling gently over which to eat first), she heard the bloke enter through the swinging plastic streamers over the door and come up behind her, standing too close, breathing, *What are ya? Ya a man or a woman?*

With her arm straight, her hand flat, she pivoted, knees bent, and cracked him from his ear to the point of his jaw, with just the amount of lift in her shoulder and thighs to have him off his feet, staggering backwards.

Neapolitan ice-cream and Chiko roll in hand, she exited through the fly curtain and out into the rain, which by then had reduced itself to a half-hearted mango breathed shower.

Scorpio to Venus: Love song 1977

I always think of my Sandman Holden Ute as a dyke vehicle.

I've perfected the finger-wave to acknowledge its country-boy rellies you find ubiquitous on Route 83 out of the Isa or even on the narrow bitumen of the Newell past Goondiwindi.
But that dyke ute did us all proud at the beaches and coastal highways where dirt roads and off-road and four-wheel drive was over-kill looking for road-kill.

The first owner of my ute was a male person, Scottish descent, age 24, named Bruce. He was killed, and also his mother (no name given) when they were on the unstable road shoulder near Boulia taking a breather in the noise of the night silence. They heard one road-train, didn't realise it was two, passing on top of them, and stepped back too late.

But the ute was fine, not a scratch or a bruise and still as red and gorgeous as it had ever been. The thrill of the V8 on ignition, new radial tyres, radial tuned transmission. How could I not think of her as one of us.

The Sandman was not your average ute. It's true, it was not yet the Kingswood, but there was no sense of playing an instrument with one string. That engine was the whole four piece rock band, right there, in the interplay of clutch, accelerator and brake.

The thing you should know, much more than your own discomfort, and theoretically true, is that with a dyke holding the key, that ute could pull the chicks.

That ute was a chick-magnet, bringing with it its own cloud of dust. And with two girls up front, it focussed the attention of the boys with their surfboards, faded board shorts, and broken boxes of *Mr Zogs Quick Humps Sex Wax* in the pockets of their windcheaters.

I kept that beauty of a ute as clean as Bruce's mother had left it, as spic and span as any house-proud dyke with her eye on a good thing.

Where will my atoms go when I die? They'll mix and meld with the Sandman, ride that V8 rumble through Scorpio to Venus.

Plot

The only time I inadvertently got engaged, I resisted the lure, cast out by my mother, of a wedding gift of a brand new Singer sewing machine. If I went through with it all.

You will always be able to make a living she said,
if the marriage doesn't last.

Use a very sharp knife

Clare was my Aunt, never auntie,
and Stel was her *friend* (spoken with a strange emphasis)
they were aware of the benefits in courtship
of keeping your elbows nice
so when moisturising also pay attention to the elbows
(not sure why knees didn't merit this concern).
Also, the critical importance of being able to maintain decorum
by peeling and eating an orange in public
use a very sharp knife, keep the orange peel strip the same width and turn
the orange carefully so that the whole peel comes off in a delicate spiral
if you only have a blunt knife pick a different fruit

In 1963, *Tom Jones* was a risqué movie, and they asked me curiously
what I thought of the protagonist played by Albert Finney—
in 1963 I didn't know what they were asking

Getting through Sunday

they sit around the kitchen table as if the Presbyterian minister
had taken his turn for Sunday lunch
six of them, boys with hair wet-combed,
girls in Sunday frocks so they look properly like girls,
elbows tucked in, sitting backs straight but heads lowered,
masticating with mouths closed, silent
tough mutton, cold pudding, passing the salt,
then the custard jug, eyes on their no-scraps-left plates

eye contact makes you visible,
when seconds are offered you can choose—
no to keep your head safely down, *yes* to be briefly seen,
but carefully timed to incur no prejudice

chewing on under the Gypsy Moth conversation flight path,
adults snipe at each other from opposite ends of the table

circling, lifting, gunning, coming in from behind,
materialising out of the centre of the sun,

floating down from above

from the get-go

from the get-go
I felt sorry for him—
a bloke with intention ...
but I was a dyke
with attitude

Nancy revisited

I'll cut off all my auburn fringe and be a shearer too says Nancy

Willie says *but you can't, you're a girl and girls are designed to sleep with and leave*

and so, reader, we leave Nancy, shorn to be a shearer
in dungarees and work-boots, and Willy, gobsmacked that a girl,
hidden from the gaze of men, can work the boards

after a kiss

Notes

'Robbie Burns may not have been completely right ...'
Epigraph: 'To a louse' in *The Complete Works of Robert Burns*, William P. Nimmo, Edinburgh 1866, p. 31.

'Sea Horse Ball'
A ball presented by the Sea Horse Society whose aim is to bring cross dressers and transgender people together socially in a safe venue, to provide support for them, their partners and families, and to promote better understanding to the wider community.

'to lesbian (i)'
Macquarie Encyclopedic Dictionary, 1990. The Macquarie Library, Macquarie University NSW

'Situation'
Tancredi: see Rossini's opera *Jerusalem Delivered*. Cixous tries to avoid the trapping of ourselves in the conscription of the label 'woman' and is fascinated by Rossini's taking a male character, Tancredi, and making Tancredi a woman, sung by a woman.

'She can only be this woman'
The Ministry of Utmost Happiness, Arundhati Roy, Hamish Hamilton 2017, p. 19: 'The woman Aftab followed could dress as she was dressed and walk the way she did only because she wasn't a woman.'

'Whatever she wants'
The Ministry of Utmost Happiness, Arundhati Roy, Hamish Hamilton 2017, p. *19:* 'Whatever she was, Aftab wanted to be her.'

'Homing'
This is an erasure poem from '*My Country*' by Dorothea Mackellar in *Australian Poetry Since 1788*, Geoffrey Lehmann and Robert Gray (eds), UNSW Press 2011.

'He went to Brighton Beach'
This is an erasure poem from '*The Sick Stockrider*' by Adam Lindsay Gordon on the theme of the quote: 'At dawn the next morning Gordon went to the beach at Brighton and shot himself.' See '*Gordon, Adam Lindsay (1833–1870)*' by Leonie Kramer, *Australian Dictionary of Biography* Vol 4, MUP 1972.

'Peripatetic Affair'
This is an erasure poem from AB Paterson's '*Clancy of the Overflow*', in *Australian Poetry Since 1788,* Geoffrey Lehmann and Robert Gray (eds), UNSW Press 2011, p. 96.

'Scorpio to Venus'
Mr Zogs Sex Wax was introduced in 1972 and quickly became the first choice for professional surfers.

'Nancy revisited'
Re-envisioning '*The Banks of the Condamine'*, Anonymous, *Australian Poetry from 1788*, Geoffrey Lehmann and Robert Gray (eds), UNSW Press 2011, p. 56.

Afterword

The theorising of gender has moved on since I completed my doctoral thesis *Acting Like a Girl* in 1994. Now in 2018 we can look at gender through the lens of LGBTIQ possibilities, enjoying the fluidity and dissonance of mismatches between sex, gender and desire.

This poetry collection was inspired by my thesis, which considered how the performance of gender and sexuality by young women can recognise cultural marginalisation, and can be at odds with the 'normal', the legitimate, the dominant.

Acts of resistance and dissent in asserting our agency to nonconform make great stories and interesting poetry. And in telling some of these stories we assert our freedom to make poetry resist the violence of immutable masculinity and femininity.

And, caution, do not assume that the poems are necessarily autobiographical.

Acknowledgements

Thanks to the Canberra poetry community for support, opportunity and encouragement over the last few years.

Some of the poems have been previously published:

'Girls who are taken by flannies' *Australian Poetry Journal* 8.2 Spoken, December 2018

'How do we imagine what we can't imagine?' *Wild* poems selected and edited by Joan Fenney, Ginninderra Press 2018

'High point of the season' *Hecate* Issue 44, University of Queensland 2018

'Toad princes' *Other Terrain* Issue 6, Swinburne University 2018

'Edit' Spineless Wonders, performed at Little Fictions Redfern, 2018

Sandra Renew's current project is on the interrogation of gender presentation and the myriad options and choices we make in living and performing our gender, sexuality and desire. Her published poetry references our contemporary world since the 1960s, including war, guns, gender, refugees, and gay and lesbian politics.

She has recently had poems published in *Hecate* (University of Queensland), *Meniscus* and *Axon* (University of Canberra), *Backstory* and *Other Terrain* (Swinburne University), *Verity La,* and *Spineless Wonders*. Her tanka and tanka prose is published internationally, and she has poems included in anthologies in Australia and UK.

Sandra co-edits (with Moya Pacey) the on-line women's poetry journal, *Not Very Quiet* and organises monthly poetry readings for women poets at *That Poetry Thing at Smiths Alternative* in Canberra. She has been a featured poet at the National Folk Festival in Canberra in 2017, 2018, and 2019 and curates the performance of *Women out of Line(s)*.

2019 Editions
Palace of Memory **Paul Hetherington**
Acting Like a Girl **Sandra Renew**
Summer Haiku **Owen Bullock**
Strange Stars: A Queer Poetry Anthology **Various**
A Common Garment **Anita Patel**
A Coat of Ashes **Jackson**
Some Sketchy Notes on Matter **Angela Gardner**
The Question Nest **Peter Bakowski**
Breathing in Stormy Seasons **Stephanie Green**
Strange Creatures **Alyson Miller**

2018 Editions
The Uncommon Feast **Eileen Chong**
Inlandia **KA Nelson**
Peripheral Vision **Martin Dolan**
The Love of the Sun **Matt Hetherington**
Moving Targets **Jen Webb**
Things I Have Thought to Tell You Since I Saw You Last **Penelope Layland**
The Many Uses of Mint **Ravi Shankar**
Abstractions **Various**
ACE: Arresting, Contemporary stories by Emerging Writers **Various**

all titles available from
www.recentworkpress.com

www.ingramcontent.com/pod-product-compliance
Lightning Source LLC
Chambersburg PA
CBHW032051290426
44110CB00012B/1046